Curriculum Candy

Curriculum Candy is an easy-to-use source of reading and writing projects that help teachers differentiate instruction. This new version features updated language, activities, and references to fit the needs of today's classrooms.

Covering categories such as novels, poetry, fairy tales, autobiographies, nonfiction, and more, each page provides a menu of four in-depth, open-ended, and varied project choices, allowing students to pick a project that fits their interests, ability level, and learning style. Each menu is graphically interesting and perfect to post on a bulletin board or in a learning center for enrichment or extra credit choices.

This enriching, student-centered resource takes the guess work out of differentiating lesson extensions and is a must have for all teachers and gifted and talented specialists looking to challenge students with a variety of strengths and interests in one classroom.

Laurie Stolmack Eaton is a retired teacher and gifted and talented specialist with more than 35 years of experience. She has a master's degree and endorsement in gifted and talented education. Laurie has taught in elementary and middle school, as well as serving as a gifted and talented specialist in the Denver Public Schools Gifted and Talented Department. She has worked with gifted specialists, teachers, and administrators throughout the district to find ways to identify and meet the needs of gifted students, to provide professional development on how to differentiate lessons, and to research, develop, and provide resources that tie in to the district curriculum. This book was specifically designed to enhance the literacy curriculum by providing student choice and project-based activities.

Curriculum Candy
Student Choice Projects that Sweeten the Literacy Curriculum

3rd edition

Laurie Stolmack Eaton

Routledge
Taylor & Francis Group

NEW YORK AND LONDON

Designed cover image: Getty images

Third edition published 2025

by Routledge
605 Third Avenue, New York, NY 10158

and by Routledge
4 Park Square, Milton Park, Abingdon, Oxon, OX14 4RN

Routledge is an imprint of the Taylor & Francis Group, an informa business

First edition published by Prufrock Press 2012

ISBN: 9781032868103 (hbk)
ISBN: 9781032867380 (pbk)
ISBN: 9781003529316 (ebk)

DOI: 10.4324/9781003529316

Typeset in Adobe Caslon Pro
by Deanta Global Publishing Services, Chennai, India

Table of Contents

Author's Note

A large part of my job involves providing teachers and gifted and talented specialists with enriching resources that tie directly to the district curriculum. When approaching the literacy curriculum, I was at a loss when it came to finding books with resource activities that were in-depth, project-based, provided choice, and tied directly to the topics of study. Because I didn't see exactly what I was looking for, and because I needed a product that met the district standards and 21st-century skills guidelines, I decided to put together my own activity book.

I wrote *Curriculum Candy: Student Choice Projects that Sweeten the Literacy Curriculum* as a one-stop resource that would tie directly into both the 21st-century skills standards and the reading, writing, and communication standards set by my school district (Colorado Department of Education, 2020), standards similar to those used in school districts nationwide.

Students with a wide range of abilities, strengths, and motivation levels really enjoy the activities included in this book. Each page provides a menu that gives students four choices. My students truly get excited about choosing their own individual projects, rather than being assigned the same ones as other students. They put more thought and effort into their projects, and they also like seeing how the same topic can be presented in many different ways. During presentations, students are inspired to try other project ideas, so

I post the project menus on the classroom wall and leave them there all year so that students who are interested in doing extra-credit assignments can choose from all of the options.

Curriculum Candy includes menus in each of the following categories:

- ➤ autobiography,
- ➤ researching and informing,
- ➤ poetry,
- ➤ novels,
- ➤ fairy tales,
- ➤ nonfiction communications,
- ➤ descriptive communications,
- ➤ narrative communications,
- ➤ persuasive communications, and
- ➤ expository communications.

These categories are found in many districts' literacy standards, as well as on many standardized writing tests. The menus are quite varied, including activities such as writing, creating, speaking, acting, analyzing, evaluating, researching, applying knowledge, and more. They include both individual and small-group projects, and many are adaptable for either format. The activities can be done in class or as long-term homework projects. The menus also work well in homeschool settings.

When parents of my students ask if there is anything that their child can do for enrichment or to extend learning, I point them to *Curriculum Candy* and encourage them to have their child complete additional activities from the book's menus.

Many gifted resource teachers use *Curriculum Candy* menus to meet the specific needs of their advanced students. They use the menus to extend the curriculum for students who are able to go into more depth. At the same time, the flexibility of the projects means that students at any level can benefit.

I hope you find *Curriculum Candy* as useful in your classroom as I have found it in mine!

—*Laurie Stolmack Eaton*

Introduction

21st-Century Skills for Reading, Writing, and Communicating

Today's students need a repertoire of knowledge and skills that are more diverse, complex, and integrated than those of any previous generation. Communication is a very important aspect of reading and writing, and effective communication skills are necessary in students' everyday lives. Such skills are essential to 21st-century learners, whether they go on to college, the workforce, or technical training. *Curriculum Candy: Student Choice Projects that Sweeten the Literacy Curriculum* takes these 21st-century skills into consideration in its array of activities. These skills enable students to learn and set goals independently and collaboratively. The categories below summarize the skills that students must develop in today's 21st-century classrooms and were informed by my own district's standards (Colorado Department of Education, 2020) and by the 21st Century Skills put out by Career and Technical Education (CTE) (2024).

Critical Thinking and Reasoning

In order for students to be successful and powerful readers, writers, and communicators, they must incorporate critical thinking and reasoning skills.

DOI: 10.4324/9781003529316-1

Students need to be able to successfully argue a point, justify reasoning, evaluate for a purpose, infer to predict and draw conclusions, problem solve, and understand and use logic to inform critical thinking.

Information Literacy

The student who is information literate accesses information efficiently and effectively by reading and understanding content from a range of informational texts and documents, both traditional and electronic. This involves evaluating information critically and thoroughly distinguishing among facts, points of view, and opinions.

Collaboration

Reading, writing, and communicating must encompass collaboration skills. Students should be able to collaborate with each other in multiple settings: in peer groups, one on one, in front of an audience, in large- and small-group settings, and with people from backgrounds different from their own.

Self-Direction

Students who read, write, and communicate independently portray self-direction by using metacognitive skills. These important skills are a learner's automatic awareness of knowledge and ability to understand, control, and manipulate his or her own cognitive processes. These skills are important not only in school, but also throughout life, enabling the student to learn and set goals independently.

Invention

Invention is one of the key components of creating an exemplary writing piece or synthesizing information from multiple sources. Invention takes students to a higher level of metacognition while they explore literature and write about their experiences by forming new ideas.

Communication

In the age of text-based communication (including texting, emails, and social media) it's never been more important for students to learn how to convey their thoughts in a way that others can understand them. Students need to learn how to communicate effectively. That includes minimizing tangents, speaking directly to an idea, and checking other participants to make sure they're engaged. When they master the art of effective communication, students can streamline their ideas and make a positive impression on those around them.

Creativity and Divergent Thinking

Curriculum Candy provides students with the opportunity to look at unique situations and come up with alternative outcomes by combining research with creative thinking. The book poses real prompts—prompts that have many possible answers—that lead to discovery, better insight, and active involvement in subject matter. The book presents prompts that ask students to consider cause-and-effect relationships, as well as prompts that demand a wide variety of responses and activities—including discussion, debate, prototype, dramatization, and other forms of artistic expression. These activities offer opportunities for students to demonstrate fluent, flexible, original, and elaborate thinking.

Fluency

The activities in this book foster fluency, or the ability to think of or consider multiple ideas and possibilities. With the menus in this book, students are encouraged to come up with alternate ideas, answers, solutions, and outcomes.

Flexibility

Flexibility—the ability to think of varied ideas—is encouraged by the activities in this book, which prompt students to look at things from different angles and perspectives.

Originality

Students, through the menus in this book, develop their ability to think of unusual ideas. *Curriculum Candy* encourages students to produce novel responses and ideas.

Elaboration

By completing the activities found in this book, students will develop elaboration, or the ability to add to ideas in order to improve them. This book challenges students to explain their ideas or include additional information.

Evaluating Creative Thinking

The rubric on page 8 can be used to evaluate students with regard to the facets of creativity discussed here. As with any rubric, it will be helpful to thoroughly review the components in question with students prior to scoring, grading, or evaluation.

The Importance of Reading, Writing, and Communicating

English Language Arts Standards

In recent years, many school districts have moved toward an integrated model of literacy that includes reading, writing, and communicating. Literacy building has become a shared responsibility for all content-area teachers. Research skills are now integrated across the standards and across the grade levels in many school districts. There has been a big shift in the standards in that the emphasis, particularly in the upper grades, is now on writing to argue, inform, and explain—writing, in other words, with purpose.

Curriculum Candy was written with consideration of all content areas. Research skills, increasingly valuable and emphasized in our information-driven society, are addressed in their own section, Researching and Informing, and many prompts featured on menus in other sections also require research.

Standardized writing tests focus predominantly on four types of writing: descriptive, narrative, persuasive, and expository. *Curriculum Candy* includes menus for each of these four types of writing, along with writing to argue, writing to inform, and writing to explain. When writing this book, the standards set forth by the International Reading Association and the National Council of Teachers of English (reaffirmed 2012) were taken into account:

> ➤ Students adjust their use of spoken, written, and visual language (e.g., conventions, style, vocabulary) to communicate effectively with a variety of audiences and for different purposes.

Creativity Rubric

Name: _____ Date: _____

Score	3 (Excellent)	2 (Good)	1 (Needs Improvement)
Fluency (Multiple Ideas)	Evidence of ability to come up with a wide variety of ideas, answers, solutions, and outcomes above and beyond those of others.	Evidence of ability to come up with a wide variety of ideas, answers, solutions, and outcomes at or slightly above those of peers.	Little evidence of ability to come up with a wide variety of ideas, answers, solutions, and outcomes.
Flexibility (Varied Ideas)	Evidence of resourcefulness, versatility, adaptability, and freedom above and beyond those of others.	Evidence of resourcefulness, versatility, adaptability, and freedom at or slightly above those of peers.	Little evidence of resourcefulness, versatility, adaptability, and freedom.
Originality (Unique Ideas)	Evidence of unique, eccentric, unusual, and inventive thinking above and beyond that of others.	Evidence of unique, eccentric, unusual, and inventive thinking at or slightly above that of peers.	Little evidence of unique, eccentric, unusual, and inventive thinking.
Elaboration (Expanded Ideas)	Evidence of a concern for detail above and beyond that of others.	Evidence of a concern for detail at or slightly above that of peers.	Little evidence of a concern for detail.

Total: _____

➤ Students employ a wide range of strategies as they write and use different writing process elements appropriately to communicate with different audiences for a variety of purposes.

➤ Students conduct research on issues and interests by generating ideas and questions and by posing problems. They gather, evaluate, and synthesize data from a variety of sources (e.g., print and nonprint texts, artifacts, people) to communicate their discoveries in ways that suit their purpose and audience.

➤ Students use a variety of technological and information resources (e.g., libraries, databases, computer networks, video) to gather and synthesize information and to create and to communicate knowledge.

➤ Students use spoken, written, and visual language to accomplish their own purposes (e.g., for learning, enjoyment, persuasion, and the exchange of information) (p. 3).

Oral Presentation Skills

In keeping with the rising priority of 21st-century skills requiring excellent interpersonal communication, many of the activities in this book ask students to present their products to the class or to make an oral presentation. The rubric on page 10 can be used to evaluate students. It is helpful to review with students the categories and criteria, as well as examples.

Differentiating for Areas of Strength

This book is meant to make teachers' efforts to differentiate in the classroom as easy and as far reaching as possible. The ideas of Carol Ann Tomlinson (1999) were valuable influences in the writing of this book, which strives to provide students encouragement, opportunities, and rigor in the areas listed below.

Oral Presentation Skills Rubric

Name: _____ Date: _____ Score: _____

Project Description: _____

	3 (Excellent)	2 (Good)	1 (Needs Improvement)
Delivery	Holds attention of entire audience with the use of direct eye contact, seldom looking at notes. Speaks with fluctuation in volume and inflection to maintain audience interest and emphasize key points.	Consistently uses direct eye contact with audience, but still returns to notes. Speaks with satisfactory variation of volume and inflection.	Displays minimal eye contact with audience, and reads mostly from notes. Speaks in uneven volume with little or no inflection.
Content/ Organization	Provides clear purpose and topic; offers correct and pertinent examples, facts, and statistics; and supports conclusions and ideas with evidence.	Has a somewhat clear purpose and topic; includes some examples, facts, and statistics that support the topic; and includes some data or evidence that supports conclusions.	Attempts to define purpose and topic. Provides weak examples, facts, and statistics that do not adequately support the topic. Includes very thin data or evidence.
Enthusiasm/ Audience Awareness	Demonstrates strong enthusiasm about the topic during entire presentation. Significantly increases audience understanding and knowledge of topic. Convinces audience to recognize the validity and importance of the topic.	Shows some enthusiastic feelings about the topic. Raises audience understanding and awareness of most points.	Shows little or mixed feelings about the topic being presented. Raises audience understanding and knowledge of some points.

Creativity

- ➤ Encourages fluency, flexibility, originality, and elaboration through open-ended classroom activities and products.
- ➤ Provides opportunities for real-world investigations and experiences.
- ➤ Provides opportunities for creative problem solving and divergent thinking techniques.
- ➤ Provides opportunities for students to connect prior knowledge to new learning experiences and to establish relationships across disciplines.
- ➤ Integrates creative thinking skills and problem-solving strategies with solid learning content.

General Intellectual Ability

- ➤ An emphasis is placed on higher level abstract thinking and problem solving.
- ➤ An emphasis is placed on students' interests, learning styles, and strengths.
- ➤ Provides opportunities for independent and small-group projects and investigations.
- ➤ Projects provided utilize concept-based thematic instruction.

Specific Academics

- ➤ Product options develop analytical and critical thinking skills.
- ➤ Projects provided encourage participation in creative writing opportunities, debate, and advanced literacy activities.
- ➤ An emphasis is placed on open-ended problems with multiple solutions or multiple paths to solutions.
- ➤ Technology use is encouraged.

➤ The regular school curriculum is extended to provide greater depth and breadth than is typically available.

➤ Projects provided aid students in organizing information, writing, and developing projects.

Visual, Spatial, and Performing Arts

➤ Multiple intelligence strength areas are embedded.

➤ Visual-spatial strategies in the content areas are embedded.

➤ Provides visual-spatial activities/products to improve performance in weaker academic area(s).

➤ Helps students transfer abstract thinking into a variety of forms of expression.

➤ Uses choice in student assignments so students can use their strengths to demonstrate their knowledge.

Interpersonal/Leadership Ability

➤ Encourages a social climate within the classroom that fosters acceptance and appreciation for the strengths of all students.

➤ Provides learning opportunities for students to work cooperatively with peers of like abilities and interests.

➤ Builds on students' strengths.

➤ Develops high-level effective communication.

➤ Supports a positive environment in which students respect and encourage others.

Ways to Integrate Activities Into Your Classroom

There are numerous ways in which you can work this book's activities into your classroom, whether you wish to extend the content, build certain skills, or allow students to pursue their own passions. Many teachers combine these integration strategies and custom fit the menus included in this book to their classrooms. However you implement these activities into your classroom, it is recommended that you provide students some measure of assessment or feedback. I have included the project assessment form (page 15) that I use in my own classroom, should you wish to use it. The following ideas are suggestions for how the activities may be used in your classroom.

Content Extension

Use projects to add or go beyond the existing curriculum. Activities may be completed in the classroom or in a separate setting.

Advanced Product Development/Presentations

Students create projects to demonstrate and extend what they learned as a result of content and process.

Accommodations for Strength Area(s)

Projects can be used to accommodate strength areas (e.g., content acceleration, advanced content pacing, independent study).

Alternative Instructional Strategies

Tasks can be assigned to students after mastery of content has been demonstrated in order to promote high-quality and rigorous academic learning. Project tasks replace some or all of the lessons being taught to the whole group.

Contract Learning

Support differentiation by organizing student responsibilities for replacement tasks. The student can sign a contract indicating what activities will replace regular curriculum. Projects provide opportunities for students to work independently with some freedom while maintaining the teacher's instructional objectives. The contract delineates what is expected and encourages students' responsibility for learning.

Curriculum Compacting

After demonstrating a level of proficiency in the basic curriculum (through preassessment or other means), a student can be allowed to exchange instructional time for other learning experiences or replacement tasks.

Content Acceleration/ Partial Acceleration

These projects remove the ceiling on what is learned. Teachers can also adjust the level to expand the content beyond the material presented, offering students the chance to pursue the subject matter beyond what is expected or to pursue their own interests.

Interest Grouping

Students can be grouped for projects according to areas of personal relevance or interest. This can be especially useful for students with high levels of interpersonal intelligence, who often flourish in atmospheres in which they are able to interact with others. Often, such grouping can also prove useful for shyer students, who may do well with students who share their interests and understand them better than others.

In-Depth Study/Individual Projects

These in-depth study projects can be included as part of a specific class assignment.

Project Assessment

Name: _____

Date: _____

Project Choice: _____

Score/Assessment: _____

Organization and Impact	No 1	Somewhat 2	Yes 3	Strong Yes 4
Was the work successful, given the purposes and goals?				
Was it easy to follow?				
Was the desired result achieved?				
Process and Product	No 1	Somewhat 2	Yes 3	Strong Yes 4
Was mastery or learning demonstrated?				
Was proper procedure followed?				
Was the product of high quality?				
Content	No 1	Somewhat 2	Yes 3	Strong Yes 4
Did the product show complexity at an appropriate level?				
Was the product on topic?				
Was the content valid?				

One thing that might have improved this project is:_____

_____

_____

One thing that I admired about this project was:_____

_____

_____

Autobiography

DOI: 10.4324/9781003529316-2

LOOKING AT YOU

Choose one activity to complete.

A Self-Portrait

Create a self-portrait. Then write a poem that describes who you really are, using poetic devices such as simile and metaphor. Combine the poem with your self-portrait.

A Review

Write a review of your life. Tell the good and the bad (pros and cons). Research a variety of reviews (e.g., movie, book, games, etc.) for style and substance. Don't forget to include a star rating (1–5 stars).

An Autobiographical Timeline

Develop an autobiographical timeline with an important event from each year of your life. Include a national or international event that happened each year, and tell why it had meaning for you, your family, or our world.

A Prediction

Predict what goals you will achieve over the next 20 years. Include major accomplishments related to career, family, and special events. Tell how you will work to achieve these goals. Present your information in written form, with visuals.

 Bonus

Pitch Your Own Project Idea for potential teacher approval.

YOU and Your LIFE

Choose one activity to complete.

Create a Social Media Account

Create a mock social media account about your life. Include pictures and information about your life. List accomplishments, interests, family, and so on.

Draw a Blueprint

Draw a blueprint of your dream bedroom. Include meaningful possessions from your past and present into your bedroom. Explain why these possessions are meaningful to you.

Write a School Memoir

Write a memoir of your school life. Include information about each year. Also include other information, such as photos, drawings, report cards, work samples, and so on.

Create a Diary from the Past

Write a diary from a time in your life other than the present. For example, create a diary from when you were in first grade or a diary of last summer. Include 5–7 days of diary entries.

✦ Bonus ✦

Pitch Your Own Project Idea for potential teacher approval.

More About You

Choose one activity to complete.

EVENTS IN YOUR LIFE

Make a list of events in your life—milestones, trips taken, happy memories, painful memories, and so on. Survey classmates to see how many others have shared some of your experiences. Summarize the results.

SMALL MOMENTS

Read a variety of memoirs, and write three memoirs of your own describing small moments in your life. Use similes and/or metaphors to make your memoir as clear as a picture.

A BOOK WITH CAPTIONS

Put together a collection of sketches and/or photographs of events that have happened in your life thus far. Turn your collection into a book or eBook with captions.

AN ABC BOOK ABOUT YOU

Create an ABC book all about you. What does each letter of the alphabet stand for in your life? Include drawings or photos, and explain how each is relevant.

  **Pitch Your Own Project Idea** for potential teacher approval.

YOU, YOU, AND YOU

Choose one activity to complete.

PERSONAL ITEMS. Choose five personal items that represent or symbolize who you are. Give a presentation in which you show each item and explain its significance in your life.

COLLAGE. Get help making a silhouette of your head. Fill it with drawings, captions, and pictures that describe you.

DESCRIBE IT. Choose a moment in time that you will never forget. Remember where you were. Remember what thoughts and emotions were running through your mind. Describe this moment in as much detail as possible.

BREAKING NEWS. "Breaking News" stories pop up all over social media and television. They are up-to-the-minute reports that keep the public informed. Create a breaking news story about yourself. It can be from the past, present, or future. Include a photo, headlines, and details.

✦ **Bonus** ✦

Pitch Your Own Project Idea for potential teacher approval.

Tell and Show

CHOOSE ONE ACTIVITY TO COMPLETE.

SELECT A PHOTO

Select a meaningful photograph from a family event, and share it with the class. Write a memoir explaining the photo and telling why it is meaningful to you.

SHARE A SONG

Select a song that reflects something you have experienced. Explain what effect the song has on you when you listen to it, and why. Share the song with your classmates.

SHARE A SPECIAL PLACE

Create a model or a map of a special place in your life. Explain what this place is like and why it is important to you.

FAMILY VACAY

Tell about a great family trip. Include location, things to do, where to eat/stay, etc. Present on Instagram or another favorite social media platform.

✦ Bonus ✦

Pitch Your Own Project Idea for potential teacher approval.

IF YOU

Choose one activity to complete.

Memoir

If you could add one person to your family, who would it be? Write an imagined memoir telling about this person, and explain how this person is an asset to your family.

A Powerful Speech

If you could make one rule that everyone in the world had to follow, what rule would you make, and why? Give a powerful, emotional speech that will sway people to agree with you.

You Won!

You just won a million dollars. You can spend it on anything or anyone but yourself. How would you spend it? Tell how much money you would leave to each person, organization, and so on, and explain your choices.

Singing Telegram

If you had the opportunity to get a message across to a large group of people, what would your message be? Present your message in the form of a singing telegram.

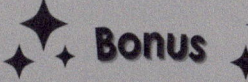

✦ Bonus ✦

Pitch Your Own Project Idea for potential teacher approval.

Researching and Informing

DOI: 10.4324/9781003529316-3

Attention Please

CHOOSE ONE ACTIVITY TO COMPLETE.

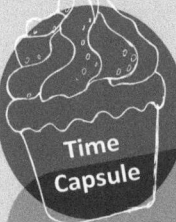

Time Capsule

If you were given the task of adding to a time capsule to be opened in 100 years, what 10 items would you include? List the items and tell why each item is significant to our time in history.

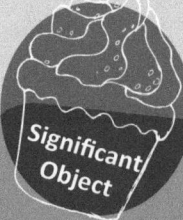

Significant Object

Create a true story around a historical object from United States History (e.g. Neil Armstrong's space suit, Lincoln's hat, etc.) Examine events, people, and places that lead to the significance of this object.

Create a Ballad

After carefully looking at the words and the meaning of "The Star Spangled Banner", create a new ballad for the 21st century.

Interview

Interview someone who has some familiarity with an event from the past—a war, a historic election, a march or protest, a history-making concert, and so on. Prepare questions to ask, but also follow up with other questions as you listen. Record the interview. Create a presentation for the class sharing what you learned.

✦ Bonus ✦

Pitch Your Own Project Idea for potential teacher approval.

Design and Make It

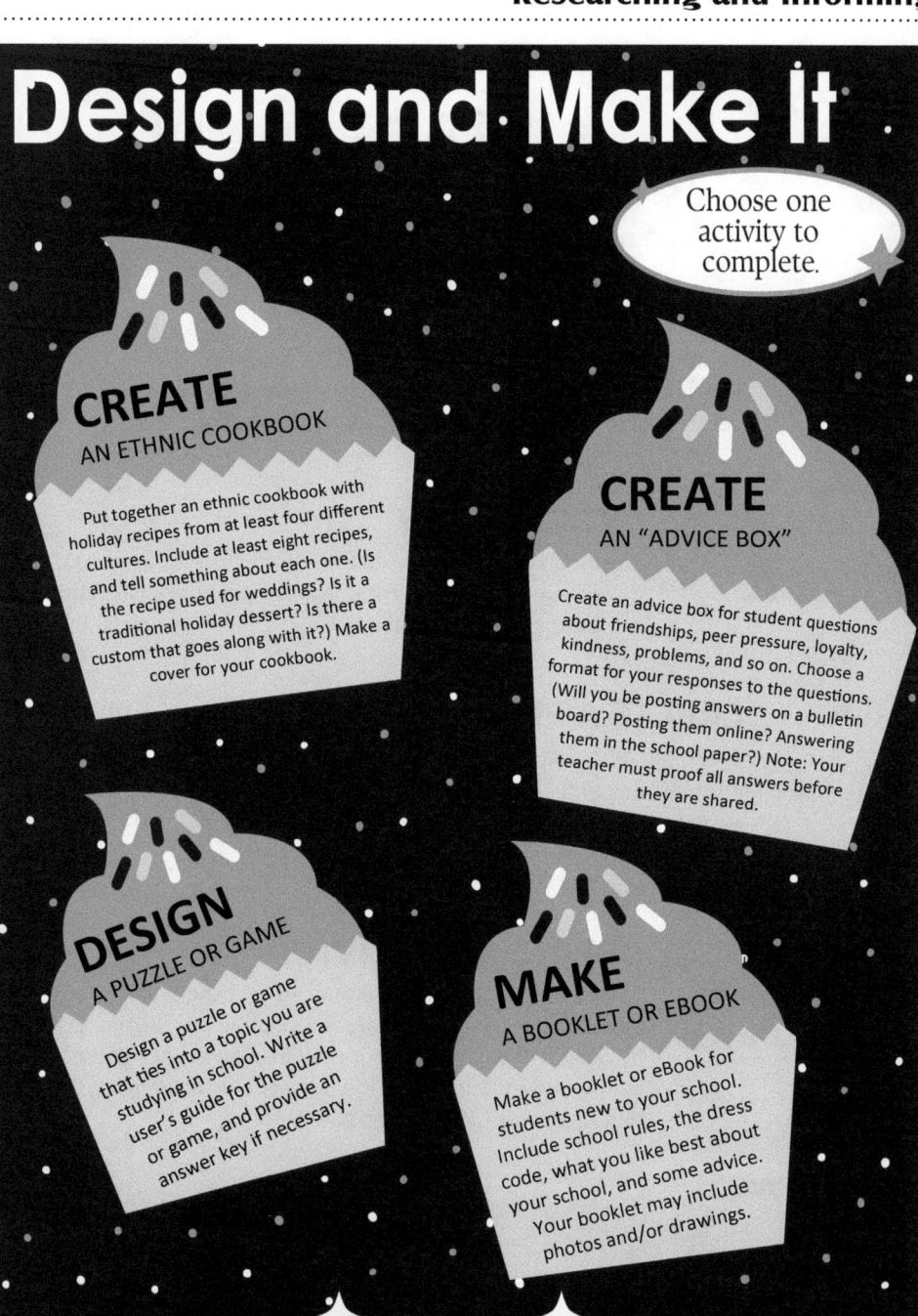

Choose one activity to complete.

CREATE
AN ETHNIC COOKBOOK

Put together an ethnic cookbook with holiday recipes from at least four different cultures. Include at least eight recipes, and tell something about each one. (Is the recipe used for weddings? Is it a traditional holiday dessert? Is there a custom that goes along with it?) Make a cover for your cookbook.

CREATE
AN "ADVICE BOX"

Create an advice box for student questions about friendships, peer pressure, loyalty, kindness, problems, and so on. Choose a format for your responses to the questions. (Will you be posting answers on a bulletin board? Posting them online? Answering them in the school paper?) Note: Your teacher must proof all answers before they are shared.

DESIGN
A PUZZLE OR GAME

Design a puzzle or game that ties into a topic you are studying in school. Write a user's guide for the puzzle or game, and provide an answer key if necessary.

MAKE
A BOOKLET OR EBOOK

Make a booklet or eBook for students new to your school. Include school rules, the dress code, what you like best about your school, and some advice. Your booklet may include photos and/or drawings.

Bonus

Pitch Your Own Project Idea for potential teacher approval.

CREATE!!
CHOOSE ONE ACTIVITY TO COMPLETE.

CREATE A DOCUMENTARY

Create a short documentary film about an issue in your school or your community. Choose a subject you feel strongly about or would like to learn more about.

CREATE A TOY

Create an original toy. Tell the significance of this toy. Then develop a user's guide for it. Make sure your instructions are clear and easy to follow.

CREATE A PICTURE BOOK

Create an alphabet picture book on a specific topic you are interested in (e.g., baseball, an endangered species, fashion, soccer, kinds of transportation). Include pictures and facts for each letter of the alphabet.

CREATE AN ACTIVITY

The PE teacher has just announced that there will be a new event for field day this year, and you will be the one to design it. What is the name of your new field ay event? Describe this event, and explain why it is a perfect field ay activity. Give a demonstration of this event.

✦ Bonus ✦
Pitch Your Own Project Idea for potential teacher approval.

YOUR VIEWS

CHOOSE ONE ACTIVITY TO COMPLETE.

LEAD A PANEL DISCUSSION

What is the approximate budget spent on space exploration? Is space exploration worth the money we spend on it? Provide classmates with both the pros and the cons of space exploration, and set up a panel discussion on the topic.

DIAGRAM IT

Would you rather float down the Amazon River or the Nile River? Gather information on both rivers, and write an essay stating the reasons for your choice. Create a Venn diagram showing the similarities and differences.

PRESENT IT

What if the Earth didn't have a moon? What effects would this have on the Earth? Create a presentation showing the relationship between the Earth and the moon.

DESIGN A PROMOTIONAL CAMPAIGN

"Zoos do more harm than good." Do you agree with this statement? Research this topic and design a promotional campaign for or against zoos.

✦ **Bonus** ✦ **Pitch Your Own Project Idea for potential teacher approval.**

Creativity COUNTS

Demonstrate an Activity

A proverb is a short but memorable saying that expresses what many would believe is a truth about life (e.g., "Don't judge a book by its cover").Choose a proverb and create a cartoon strip that illustrates its meaning. Be sure that your cartoon strip tells a story and that the message at the end is clear.

Make a Reel

Think of a trip or a holiday that was special to you, and make a reel to commemorate it. Include photos related to the trip or holiday with facts about it and what made it memorable. (Reel creators: Instagram, Canva, etc.)

Illustrate a Song

Choose a favorite song, and print out the lyrics. Then illustrate the lyrics in visual form, such as a drawing, a 3-D model, a collage, a painting, and so on. Write a paragraph describing how your illustration relates to the song lyrics.

Play with Proverbs

Present a "how-to" demonstration to the class. Show how to make, do, or repair something. Try to choose something that is not familiar to many students. The activity should be simple enough to describe in 5–10 steps.

✦ Bonus ✦
Pitch Your Own Project Idea for potential teacher approval.

POINT OF VIEW

GO GREEN

Create a list of things that hurt the environment. Then take a look at your school. How "green" is it? Make a list of actions your school could take to be more environmentally friendly. Write a letter to your principal to persuade him or her to help put your plan into action.

MAKE A POSTER

Create a poster that encourages others to do something important (e.g., recycle newspapers, drive the speed limit, eat healthy foods, donate to a charity, volunteer to help a cause). Make sure your poster includes persuasive reasons for taking action.

THE PLEDGE

Read the Pledge of Allegiance. Look up the meaning of the words Pledge, Allegiance, Republic, Nation, Indivisible, Liberty, and Justice. Rewrite the Pledge of Allegiance using simpler terms, to help younger students understand its meaning (e.g., Pledge = Promise).

LOOK AT BOTH SIDES

Write two different papers, each arguing a different side of the same issue. In one paper, defend one point of view. In the other paper, take the opposite view.

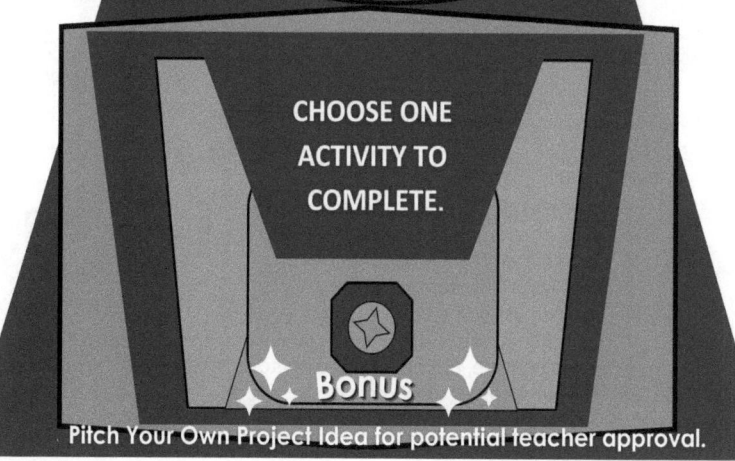

CHOOSE ONE
ACTIVITY TO
COMPLETE.

Bonus

Pitch Your Own Project Idea for potential teacher approval.

Choose one activity to complete.

Critique a Work of Art

Find out more about a particular work of art. Then critique it, including your interpretation of its meaning. Also provide information about the artist and the media used. Include samples of the artist's work.

Write an Author Review

Research an author you like. Find out more about his or her life, writing style, types of books written, and so on. Present your findings in the form of a commercial advertisement endorsing the author's books. Your commercial can be presented live or using some form of technology.

Create a Timeline

Choose a product (e.g., cars, books, movies, phones) and create a timeline showing that product's evolution. Include pictures and dates.

Inventors

Find out more about an inventor. Did the person work alone? What difficulties or setbacks did he or she face? In what ways was the inventor successful? Present your findings to the class using the technology of your choice (e.g., short-form video, social networking site, online slideshow, etc.).

Bonus

Pitch Your Own Project Idea for potential teacher approval.

Find Out More

Create a Timeline

Choose a famous person or author to profile, and research that person's life. Create a timeline of major events in the individual's life. Include photos or drawings.

Compare Cinderellas

There are stories in almost every culture similar to the story of Cinderella. Do some research on fairy tales and find two tales from different parts of the world that resemble the Cinderella story. Create a Venn diagram to illustrate the similarities and differences.

Conduct an Interview

Pick a topic that interests you. Research and find an expert in that topic. Then develop 10 interview questions on the topic. Conduct your interview and share the results. You might present the interview in written form, through an audio or video recording, or with another presentation method of your choice.

Product Review

Look up and read a variety of consumer reports and reviews on products that people purchase. Pick three different products that students in your class are likely to have used (e.g., candy, games, soft drinks), and have the class rate them. (You decide on the rating scale to be used.) Write a review of each product summarizing what the class said about it in your review.

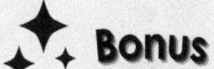 **Bonus**

Pitch Your Own Project Idea for potential teacher approval.

Choose one activity to complete.

Poetry

DOI: 10.4324/9781003529316-4

POETS & POEMS

CHOOSE ONE ACTIVITY TO COMPLETE.

WRITE THREE POEMS

Create three poems that use each of the following word combinations (the words don't have to be in the same line):

- boot, tune, fool
- but, feet, knot
- seize, fourth, arms

EXPLORE A POET YOU DON'T LIKE

Read more poetry by a poet you don't like. Figure out what it is about the poet's writing that you dislike. Choose one poem by the author, and think of ways that you would approach the same subject using your own style. Write the poem.

WRITE A POEM

Write a poem about yourself and someone you know, showing how you and that person are alike and how you are different. Include a variety of character traits in both poems. (Instead of a person you know, you may also choose a character in a book.)

RESEARCH A POET'S LIFE

Research a poet's background, and then share your thoughts about how the poet's past might be reflected in his or her poetry. Provide a sample of one of the author's poems as a point of reference.

 Bonus

Pitch Your Own Project Idea for potential teacher approval.

Roses Are Red...

Choose one activity to complete.

USE NEWS TO WRITE A POEM

Find a news or opinion article. Look for a story that has some emotional impact on you, and use that story as the basis for your poem.

ROAST YOURSELF

Write a good-natured poetic roast in which you poke fun at yourself

WRITE A LETTER POEM

Write a poem as if it were a letter to a friend. Start the poem with a piece of advice.

RECREATE POEM

Select a poem and photocopy it, also enlarging it. Cut out all of the individual words. Create a new poem from these words. (You may add additional words to complete your poem.)

 Bonus Pitch Your Own Project Idea for potential teacher approval.

Violets Are Blue...

WRITE a Poem with Strong Emotion

Write a poem that demonstrates strong emotion—but without ever directly stating what that emotion is.

CHOOSE one activity to complete.

CREATE a Mood

Choose or create music to set a mood as you recite a poem. Explain why you chose the music you did.

DRAMATIZE Poems

Present a poem that is a dramatization of a story. This can be done individually, with a partner, or with a group.

Bonus

Pitch Your Own Project Idea for potential teacher approval.

CHANGE Forms

Choose a poem and rewrite it as a story or play

Poem Explorations

Choose one activity to complete.

WRITE A POEM

Write a poem that begins with a negative image or statement and ends with a positive image or statement. You may include illustrations, if you like.

WRITE ABOUT A PLACE

Get out of the house and write in a new place, observing your surroundings. List details about the place you chose. What do you see? Smell? Taste? Hear? Feel? Be as specific as possible. Describe the place you chose in a poem. Try to create a full picture with your words.

MAKE A PICTURE BOOK

Select a poem you like. What visual images come to mind when you read this poem? Turn the poem into a picture book with visual images that are appropriate for the poem.

RECITE A POEM

Recite a poem using sound effects and props.

 Bonus

Pitch Your Own Project Idea for potential teacher approval.

Beautiful Words

Choose one activity to complete.

Advice

What is the best advice that you can give your peers (e.g., Don't be afraid to say no.) Write a poem stating your advice and the reason behind it.

A Biography

Pick a famous inventor, and create a biography poem that includes the most important information about the inventor and his or her invention.

Stamp It!

Think of something or someone you feel is important enough to be featured on a commemorative stamp. Design the postage stamp and write a poem to tell about the subject you chose.

Book Review

Pick a favorite book, and write a review in the form of a poem. Include details about both the book and the author.

★✦ **Bonus** ✦★ Pitch Your Own Project Idea for potential teacher approval.

Poetry Flair

Choose one activity to complete.

It's Rhyme Time

Create a rhyming poem that is fun, has a steady beat, and would be easy to jump rope to.

Big Bad Wolf

Write two poems about two different wolves: the wolf in The Three Little Pigs, and the wolf in Little Red Riding Hood. Along with the poems, create a venn diagram that shows the similarities and differences between the two wolves.

A Tribute

Write a tribute, in the form of a poem, about someone very special to you. Design a greeting card that includes this poem.

Scavenger Hunt

Design a scavenger hunt for your classmates that includes clues that are written in the form of poems.

✦ Bonus ✦

Pitch Your Own Project Idea for potential teacher approval.

Poetic License

Jump Rope Rhyme

Create a jump rope rhyme. Your rhyme should be easy to remember and can be repeated over and over while jumping rope. Present it while jumping rope.

Greeting Card

There are greeting cards for birthdays, anniversaries, holidays, and many other occasions. Come up with a new occasion that you feel deserves a card, and create one or more cards, each with a picture on the front and a poem inside. Be sure your idea is unique!

Rhymed Couplets

Create a series of rhymed couplets about smells that you love and smells that you hate. Research couplets to be sure that you are using the correct format.

A Sonnet

How do you feel about clowns? Explain your opinion in the form of a sonnet. Research sonnets to be sure that you are using the correct format.

Choose one activity to complete.

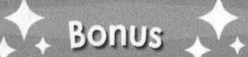

Bonus

Pitch Your Own Project Idea for potential teacher approval.

Poetry Pleasers

Choose one activity to complete.

AN ODE

Write an ode to your favorite material item (e.g., pair of jeans, teddy bear, smelly shoes).

A TELEGRAM

Choose a holiday, and write a singing telegram that describes this holiday. Present your singing telegram in your best holiday fashion, and include props.

A TRIBUTE

How do you feel about music? Write a tribute to your favorite genre of music (e.g., pop, jazz, rock, etc.) as if it were a person. Tell how you admire and honor them.

RAP IT

Describe, in a rap, one or more moments when you felt envious of someone else. Be sure your rap is appropriate for the classroom

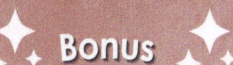 Bonus

Pitch Your Own Project Idea for potential teacher approval.

Novels

DOI: 10.4324/9781003529316-5

Novel Menu

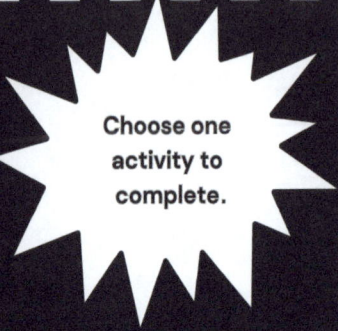

Choose one activity to complete.

Cast It

Envision that this novel will be turned into a movie. Come up with a casting list, describing what each character looks like and how they act. Include pictures of each character and possible actors who could play them.

SLIDESHOW

Develop an online slideshow presentation showing how the characters in this novel are related.

A DEFENSE

Defend this statement: This novel should be read by everyone who hates reading.

GRAFFITI

Make a graffiti wall of significant appropriate words or phrases that the characters in this novel might write. Explain how the graffiti relates to the characters in the novel.

✦ **Bonus** ✦ Pitch Your Own Project Idea for potential teacher approval.

MORE MORE MORE

CHOOSE ONE ACTIVITY TO COMPLETE.

LETTER FROM THE MAIN CHARACTER

Pretend you are the main character from this novel and write a letter to another character expressing your feelings about something that happens in the book.

A SONG OR BALLAD

Write a song or ballad about the plot, a character, or an event in this novel.

MAP

Choose a scene from this novel that you can clearly picture. Draw and label a map of that scene. Write down which passage describes your scene.

DRAMATIC SCENE

Dramatize a scene from this novel with somebody else who has read it. Write a script and have several rehearsals before presenting the scene to the class.

 **Bonus**   Pitch Your Own Project Idea for potential teacher approval.

ABOUT MY NOVEL

DESCRIBE AN EXPERIENCE

Describe an experience you've had that was like an experience of a character in this novel. You can share your experience either orally or in writing.

HOST A TALK SHOW

Along with other classmates who have read this novel, host a talk show featuring several characters. Students should play the host and characters. Write a script for what you will say so that your audience will gain a clear understanding of the novel.

CHOOSE CONFLICTS

Choose three conflicts that take place in this novel, and explain how they were resolved. Choose one solution that you wish had been handled differently and explain what you would have liked to happen.

ANOTHER POINT OF VIEW

Explain how this novel would be different if it were told from another character's point of view. Tell what character you chose, and give at least five examples of how the plot and other elements of the novel would change.

 **Bonus** Pitch Your Own Project Idea for potential teacher approval.

Choose one activity to complete.

NOVEL IDEAS

CHOOSE ONE ACTIVITY TO COMPLETE.

WHAT WOULD YOU CHOOSE?

If you had to buy something for each of the characters in the novel, what would you buy, and why? Be sure to give a detailed explanation, using evidence from the text to support your choices.

PLAYLIST

Create a playlist of at least three songs for three different events in the novel. List each song then write an explanation as to why you chose it.

INVITE A CHARACTER TO DINNER

Write a letter inviting one character from your novel to dinner. Then write a note to your parents explaining why you want to invite this character to dinner and what you have planned for their visit (e.g., food, games, subjects to discuss, etc.).

VIDEO BOOK REVIEW

Research video book reviews then create your own video book review using the technology of your choice.

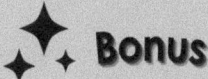 **Bonus** Pitch Your Own Project Idea for potential teacher approval.

Designing, Drawing, and Writing

CHARACTER TREE

Design and create a character tree, showing how the characters in the novel are related.

CHANGE THE LAST CHAPTER

Write a different ending to the novel you read. Include enough details to make your ending believable.

Choose one activity to complete.

A STORYBOARD

Create a large storyboard showing four different scenes from the novel. Put the scenes in sequence, and explain each scene, either in writing or in a presentation.

WRITE A CHARACTER DIARY

Choose a character from the novel, and write five diary entries as you believe the character would write them.

Bonus

Pitch Your Own Project Idea for potential teacher approval.

Telling More

CHOOSE ONE ACTIVITY TO COMPLETE.

Design an Ad Campaign

Design an advertising campaign to promote the novel you read. Create an ad for television, radio, print, and social media.

Create a Picture Book

Rewrite the novel you read as a picture book. Choose elements of the plot that young children would enjoy. Use simple vocabulary and pictures that help move the story along.

Make a Video

Read the same book as a classmate. Then make a video or do a live performance in which the two of you review the novel.

Improve the Book

The author has written to you and wants to know how his or her novel could be improved. Tell the author your advice in a letter, audio recording, or video.

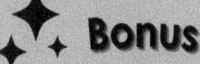 **Bonus** 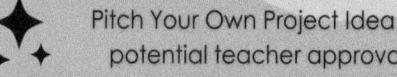 Pitch Your Own Project Idea for potential teacher approval.

BOOK TALK

Write a Letter to a Movie Producer

Imagine that you are the author of the novel you have just read. Write a letter to a movie producer trying to get him or her interested in making your book into a movie. Explain why the story, the characters, and the conflicts would make a good film.

Write a Letter to the Author

Write a letter to this book's author expressing your opinion of the book. Give reasons for why you feel as you do. Send the letter to the author.

Research a Topic

Research one specific topic that the author brings up in this novel. State the topic and present your findings and thoughts in an oral or written report.

Epilogue

Write an epilogue in which you explain what happened to the characters in this book one year after the book ends, 10 years after the book ends, and 20 years after the book ends.

Pitch Your Own Project Idea for potential teacher approval.

Choose one activity to complete.

A Look at a Book

Write a Book Summary

Summarize the plot of a book you have read. In just 10 sentences, try to capture what is most important about what happens. Create a visual representation of the plot using the medium of your choice.

Discover Figures of Speech

Find and list 15 similes and/or metaphors from this novel. Include the page where each is found.

Create a Time Capsule

Give five reasons why your novel should be included in a time capsule to be dug up in 100 years. Explain each reason.

Be a Publicist

Pretend to be a publicist for the book you have read. Write and then deliver a 60-second speech that will persuade other students that they should read the book. Write and speak persuasively, and include visuals.

Bonus

Pitch Your Own Project Idea for potential teacher approval.

Choose one activity to complete.

Fairy Tales

DOI: 10.4324/9781003529316-6

Make It Visual

Choose one activity to complete.

Make a "Wanted" Poster

Make a "Wanted" poster for one of the characters in the fairy tale. Include a picture, a physical description, the character's misdeeds, and other important information. Include the reward offered for the capture of the character.

Create a Map

Create a map or model of the setting of a chosen fairy tale, using descriptions from the story as your guide. On the inset or legend, include the pages where these descriptions were found.

Select a Container

Select a container (e.g., a cereal box, an envelope, a soup can). Decorate your container to represent major elements found in the fairy tale (e.g., setting, characters, conflicts). Then fill the container with 10 things that have a connection to the story (or that represent things that have a connection to the story). Explain your choices for both the outside and inside of your container.

Create Nicknames

Create a nickname for each of the characters in the fairy tale. Show a visual of each character and tell why you chose the nickname to represent that particular character.

Bonus

Pitch Your Own Project Idea for potential teacher approval.

Fairy Tale Exploration

Write a Letter

Write a letter (at least 10 sentences long) to one of the characters in the fairy tale asking questions, protesting a situation, and/or making a complaint or suggestion. Use the correct letter format.

Create a Diary

Choose a character from the fairy tale and write eight diary entries from that character's point of view.

Choose one activity to complete.

Explore Heroic Qualities

Select one character from the fairy tale that has the qualities of a heroine or hero. List these qualities and tell why you think they are heroic.

Change a Fairy Tale

An evil witch has just found the Fairy Godmother's wand. Pick a fairy tale and tell how the story is turned upside down now that the witch has the magic wand.

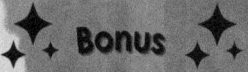

Bonus

Pitch Your Own Project Idea for potential teacher approval.

A FAIRY TALE I READ

CREATE A RESUME

Create a resume for a fairy tale character. Include a statement of the applicant's goals and a detailed account of his or her experience and outside interests. Include a list of specific jobs that your fairy tale character should apply for.

MAKE A TIMELINE

Make a timeline of 10 important events that happen in a fairy tale. Write a brief explanation of why each event is important.

CREATE A SONG

Create a song to tell about a specific fairy tale. Give your song a title, and perform it.

MAKE A LIFE-SIZED MODEL

Make a life-sized model of one of your favorite characters in the novel. Stand behind the model, as if you were the character, and describe yourself. Tell your role and how you relate to other characters in the fairy tale.

 **Bonus**

Choose one activity to complete.

Scenes, Settings, and More

Choose one activity to complete.

Setting the Scene

Build a miniature stage setting of an important scene from the fairytale. Include a written explanation of the scene's importance.

Describe a Setting

What real place does the fairy tale setting remind you of? Describe that place, and include how the real place reminds you of the setting of the fairy tale.

Highlight a Scene

Illustrate the scene that is a high point or turning point of the fairy tale. Explain why this scene is so important.

Decorate a Bedroom

If you were an interior decorator, how would you decorate the bedroom of one of the main characters in the fairy tale? Include an explanation of your design choices and why you think they would appeal to the character.

Bonus Pitch Your Own Project Idea for potential teacher approval.

BOOK LOOK

Choose one activity to complete.

Play With Words

Explain how each of the following words applies to the fairytale: commitment, urgency, anxiety, breathtaking, horrendous.

Design a Castle

Design the perfect castle for a specific fairy tale princess. The castle must be 3D, include a movable drawbridge, at least two towers, and a lawn with objects that represent the princess (e.g., a bush shaped like a glass slipper, a flag representing the princess, etc.)

Make an Online Travel Brochure

Make a travel brochure inviting tourists to visit the setting of the fairy tale. What types of activities could they take part in? Create an eye-catching title and stunning photos.

Write a Fictitious Conversation

Write and record a conversation with a character from the fairy tale. If the character could come to life, what would you ask him or her? How do you think the character would answer? Be sure to include specifics from the fairy tale that you feel are important. You can play both parts or work with a partner.

✦ Bonus ✦

Pitch Your Own Project Idea for potential teacher approval.

Ideas, Ideas

Choose one activity to complete.

Make a Collage

Make a collage that represents the fairy tale. Include a written explanation of the words and pictures selected. An online template may be used for graphics and presentation.

Merge It

Combine elements from three fairy tales to create your own tale.

Fairy Tale Sound Effects

Create sound effects to help tell a fairy tale. Choose what instrument and/or sound is most appropriate for a scene or character in the fairy tale.

Create a TV Commercial

Write and present a radio or television commercial for your fairy tale, telling your audience members why they should buy it. You may present live or share your recording.

 **Bonus**   Pitch Your Own Project Idea for potential teacher approval.

Nonfiction Communications

DOI: 10.4324/9781003529316-7

News, News, News

Choose one activity to complete.

Time Capsule

You were selected to choose an important news piece to be included in a time capsule to be dug up in 100 years. Give five reasons why you chose this specific piece of news.

New Broadcast

Watch a variety of news broadcasts both on television and online. Then tell how you would update the news to bring in younger viewers. Discuss format and content and give examples.

Report the News

Research the local and national news and select an important item from each. Present these two items as a newscaster would.

Be a Publicist

You are a publicist for a nonfiction piece that will be presented on Good Morning America. Write and deliver a 60-second speech that will persuade other students in America of the importance of this piece of work. Speak persuasively and include visuals.

 **Bonus** Pitch Your Own Project Idea for potential teacher approval.

YOU NEED TO KNOW

PUT IT ON A T-SHIRT

What is the message that the author of a book, story, or article is trying to make? Summarize the message and create a t-shirt promoting that message.

CREATE A TV COMMERCIAL

Write and present a radio or television commercial for your nonfiction piece, telling your audience members why they should read it. You may record the commercial or present it live.

EXPLORE EIGHT IDEAS

Complete each of these eight ideas, based on the nonfiction piece you have read:

This book made me:

- wish that_____.
- realize that_____.
- decide that_____.
- wonder about_____.
- see that_____.
- believe that_____.
- feel that_____.
- hope that_____.

MAKE A COLLAGE

Make a collage (using your media of choice) that represents the nonfiction piece you read. Include a written explanation of the words and pictures selected.

 Bonus

Choose one activity to complete.

Pitch Your Own Project Idea for potential teacher approval.

The Way It Is

Choose one activity to complete.

Make a Storyboard

Pick out several important events in your nonfiction piece and create a storyboard. Each scene should have a title, a summary, and a visual cue, such as an image, a symbol, or a color. Online storyboard software may be used.

Apply the Words

Explain how each of the following words applies to the nonfiction piece you read: truth, urgency, anxiety, and thoughtful.

Create a Picture Book

Rewrite the nonfiction piece you read as a picture book. Choose elements of the story and simplify them so young children will understand. Use simple vocabulary and pictures that help move the story along.

Design an Ad Campaign

Design an advertising campaign to promote the nonfiction piece you read. Explain how the piece will be promoted.

 **Bonus**

Pitch Your Own Project Idea for potential teacher approval.

Think About It

Choose one activity to complete.

History

In the year you were born, what was going on? What were people wearing? What were they talking about? What music were they listening to? Create a display that shows what was going on that year.

What Do People Think?

Take a poll to see what a sample of people think about a specific issue or problem. First write your question. Choose a question that has multiple answers. After you do the poll, summarize the results. Who did you include in the poll (Boys only? Children ages 8–10? Fifth graders? All ages?)? How many people did you include? Graph the results of your poll.

Old vs. New

Compare an older way of doing something with a newer way of doing something. For example, you might compare writing using paper and a pen with writing using a computer. Compare and contrast the two methods, orally or in writing.

A Charity or Cause

Set a goal for a cause or charity that is near and dear to you. Write an essay to explain what types of support will be necessary to reach your goal.

Pitch Your Own Project Idea for potential teacher approval.

MAKE A DIFFERENCE

NEIGHBORHOOD PRIDE

Find out the history of your neighborhood. Design a brochure with a map of the area and interesting information on its history. Cite your resources.

ENVIRONMENTAL ISSUE

Pick an environmental issue that is meaningful to you. Create a public service announcement (PSA) for radio or TV. State the problem, needs, and possible solutions for this issue.

FOR ANIMAL LOVERS

Telephone or visit your local humane society or animal shelter to get the latest statistics on the number of homeless dogs and cats in your community. Ask them about their needs and what can be done to improve the situation. Begin an information campaign of your choice.

CRIME FIGHTER

Interview police officers for suggestions and tips on how to keep from becoming a crime victim. Create a flyer teaching what you learned.

 **Bonus** Pitch Your Own Project Idea for potential teacher approval.

Choose one activity to complete.

Curriculum Candy © Prufrock Press Inc.

BECAUSE I CARE

TOLERANCE AND UNDERSTANDING

Create a pledge, similar to the Pledge of Allegiance, to help kids become more tolerant, accepting, and understanding of those who are different from them.

SURVIVAL KIT

Design a Kid Survival Kit for students new to your school. Include a map, a brief history of your school, what makes your school special, and anything else you feel a new student should know in order to feel at ease. Write a proposal to the principal promoting your kit and suggesting how it should be used.

SAFETY MATTERS

Children often get injured or get into trouble if left alone after school. Create a coloring book that teaches young children how to stay safe at home while their parents are away. Include some activities that children could do that are safe and fun.

ACCIDENT PREVENTION

Accidents are one of the leading causes of death in the United States today. Pick a topic (e.g., bike safety, fire safety) and give a speech, with visuals, describing what you can do to stay safe.

 **Bonus**

Pitch Your Own Project Idea for potential teacher approval.

CHOOSE ONE ACTIVITY TO COMPLETE.

ANSWER THE QUESTION

Choose one activity to complete.

THE UNDERGROUND RAILROAD

Was the Underground Railroad a real railroad? Research and present a map (or maps) of the Underground Railroad's route along with a monologue from a runaway slave. Include the slave's hopes, fears, and dreams.

THE MILKY WAY

Why is our galaxy called "The Milky Way Galaxy"? Answer the question and create a display of our galaxy showing what it would look like if we interpreted "The Milky Way Galaxy" in the literal sense.

BIGFOOT

Since the late 1800s, more than 3,000 sightings of Bigfoot, also called Sasquatch, have been recorded in the United States and Canada. Does Bigfoot exist? Research this topic and draw your own conclusions. Your project should include facts, resources, pictures, and your thoughts on the matter.

GRAVITY IN SPACE

Why is there no gravity in space? What if there were gravity in space? Research these two questions, then design a wordless picture book describing what would happen if there was, in fact, gravity in space. Include a written prologue to introduce the book.

 **Bonus** Pitch Your Own Project Idea for potential teacher approval.

Look It Up

Diary Excerpts

Choose a famous explorer and create five or more diary excerpts from his or her perspective. Include entries that focus on topics such as observations, daily life, dangers, and surprises.

Does Nessie Exist?

The Loch Ness Monster remains one of the world's most famous mysteries. Does it exist? Research this topic and draw your own conclusions. Your project should include facts, resources, pictures, and your thoughts on the matter.

Your Birthday Presentation

On the day that you were born, what else happened in the world? Make an online presentation that includes the day's historic events, births of famous people, a list of top songs, and so on. Use graphics, video clips, etc.

A Timeline

"Old Glory" is not just the nickname of the American Flag. There was one particular flag, the original Old Glory, that has become one of the nation's most treasured historical artifacts. Research the history of the original Old Glory, and create a timeline detailing its history.

✦ Bonus ✦

Pitch Your Own Project Idea for potential teacher approval.

Choose one activity to complete.

Descriptive Communications

DOI: 10.4324/9781003529316-8

Details, Details

Choose one activity to complete.

IDEAL VACATION

What would be your ideal vacation? Describe it, sharing details about where it would be, why you would choose that place, what you would do, when you would go, and so on. Create a travelogue of your vacation.

SUPER ME

Share the story about a time that you were brave. Describe what happened in writing, orally, or using any form of technology that you like. Include specific details.

A RITUAL

Describe a ritual that you, your family, or your friends follow. For example, do you have certain traditions at Thanksgiving? Do you and your friends have certain things you always do on birthdays? Do you need to do things in the same order every morning, getting ready for school? Describe a ritual and explain how it came about, or why you follow it. Provide a demonstration or visuals to help explain.

DREAM ROOM

Share a drawing and description of how you would remodel and redecorate your room if money were not a factor. Include colors, furniture, additions, and so on.

Bonus

Pitch Your Own Project Idea for potential teacher approval.

Off You Go!

CHOOSE ONE ACTIVITY TO COMPLETE.

KNOCK, KNOCK

You are hanging out at home on the couch, bored out of your mind. Suddenly, there is a loud knock at the front door. You open the door, and there, standing on your front porch, is a character from one of your favorite TV shows, movies, or novels, who says, "Let's go! We don't have much time!" You step outside, and you're off on an adventure. Write a letter or email to a friend describing this adventure.

WHAT GOES UP MUST COME DOWN

Get ready, because up you go. You are going to take a ride in an elevator. Where you will end up is for you to decide. But first you need to decide just where this elevator is located (e.g., a school, a boarded-up warehouse, a hospital). You start going up, and within minutes, the elevator stops, the doors open, and you're off on an adventure. Write a monologue describing your adventure.

A WRINKLE IN TIME

You open your front door to find a small package with your name on it. You open the package, and inside you find a strange wristwatch. It has a very strange watch face, not like a typical watch face with numbers or clock hands. You take the watch out of its box and put it on your wrist. You immediately feel a strange sensation, and you soon discover that this watch has strange powers. Write an advertisement describing this special watch and what happens to the person wearing it.

EVENT IN A TENT

You are looking through your binoculars when you see, off in the distance, a tent. It can be any type of tent (e.g., circus tent, teepee, wedding tent). Now you will approach the tent and step inside, and you're off on an adventure. Write a feature news piece, describing your "event in a tent" adventure. Include a headline, a lead, and the body of the news piece.

✦ Bonus ✦

Pitch Your Own Project Idea for potential teacher approval.

Tell Us About Yourself

 **Choose one activity to complete.**

A Special Place

Everyone has a special place—a place that is like no other, that holds a certain meaning to you, that makes you feel a special way. Write an essay describing your special place and why it is meaningful to you. Include a visual of this special place.

Think about a moment in time: an event that you will never forget. It may have been a special occasion, a tragedy, or even an everyday event. Describe your moment in time in detail and recite it with background music that goes along with the event.

Once Upon a Time

Behind the Uniform

You are an adult, and you have a job for which you must wear a uniform. You may be in the military, in the medical field, or even a professional athlete. Your choice! You are at work, and boy, is it an exciting day. It's a day that is out of the ordinary for you. It's a day that you will be talking about for a long time. Write a diary entry describing what your job is and what happened on this very unusual day.

First experiences are special. Think about a time that you experienced or learned something for the first time. It could be when you first rode a bike, or your first day at a new school. Maybe it was funny, scary, or exciting. Tell about the time you experienced or learned something for the first time. You can present your experience in any form (e.g., written narrative, song, poem, video).

First Experiences

 **Bonus**

Pitch Your Own Project Idea for potential teacher approval.

Let the Adventures Begin

Anything Goes

You get out of bed and head downstairs for a bowl of cereal. When you open the box of cereal, out pops a tiny leprechaun. He is no bigger than your thumb, and he's dressed in green, head to toe. He begins dancing around on the counter singing, "Top of the morning, today's your day! Whatever you want, come on, let's play!" Imagine that you can do anything you want for an entire day! Write an essay describing this day in which "anything goes," and create a timeline of the order of events.

All the World's a Stage

You are sitting in front of a stage. The theatre is packed. You are very excited, because this is something you've been waiting a long time for. You are either here to see this special event, or you may be a part of the special event. Choose the event that will be happening on stage. Write an essay describing what you saw and experienced when the curtains opened, and make a billboard to advertise this event.

An Ocean Adventure

Imagine that you are out in the middle of the ocean. Think about the floating apparatus that you're on (e.g., sailboat, raft, bathtub). Now look around you. Is anyone there with you? What do you see, hear, feel, smell, and taste as you look about? Write an article describing your experience out in the ocean.

Field of Dreams

You are standing at the edge of a field. It can be any type of field (e.g., athletic field, farm, field of daisies). Now, look down at yourself. You will find that you are dressed in an outfit appropriate for your chosen field. You are going to step onto the field and use your imagination. Visualize what happens on your field. Write an essay describing your field and explaining what took place on your field. Present your essay in costume and with props relating to your chosen field.

Choose one activity to complete.

 **Bonus** Pitch Your Own Project Idea for potential teacher approval.

THE NATURE OF IT

CHOOSE ONE ACTIVITY TO COMPLETE.

I've Got an Idea

If you were an inventor, what would you like to invent? Make a model of this invention and describe why it is necessary and how it works.

Survival

What if you were signed up for a survival course in which you had to survive in an ice cave for two weeks? Describe what you would need to take with you in order to survive, and teach a lesson on this topic.

Gone Batty

If you were a bat in a cave, what would you see/hear/taste/feel/smell? Write a collection of memoirs describing your life as a bat in a cave. Present your memoirs using background music and/or visuals to enhance your words.

Superhero to the Rescue

What might happen in your city if Superman, Batman, or another superhero resided there? What community problems could they solve, and how could they solve them? Create a cartoon book describing a situation in which the superhero could save the day.

 **Bonus**

Pitch Your Own Project Idea for potential teacher approval.

See It, Create It

Choose one activity to complete.

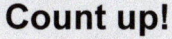

Go to your desk!

What would the perfect school desk be like? Anything goes! Describe it, draw a blueprint of it, and give it a fun name.

Shape up!

What shapes can be found in our natural environment? Create a digital scrapbook that includes pictures and descriptive captions or facts about the shape (e.g., hexagonal cells in a beehive are used for storing honey, pollen, and eggs).

Count up!

In what ways do the numbers 1–10 occur in everyday life? Create a math book for preschoolers with pictures and descriptive captions (e.g., your two eyes, three lights on a traffic light, four seasons of the year).

Make the move!

If you could rearrange the classroom desks and chairs to better suit your classroom, what changes would you make? Create a diagram showing the desk arrangement and describe how it would benefit the classroom environment.

 Bonus

Pitch Your Own Project Idea for potential teacher approval.

Narrative Communications

DOI: 10.4324/9781003529316-9

WHAT A DAY!

Choose one activity to complete.

COOL SHADES

You are on the playground swings when you notice something reflecting from the sand below. You stop swinging and reach down to discover it's a pair of glasses. You decide to try them on. You look around and the playground suddenly vanishes right before your eyes. Create a cartoon showing what you now see and your reaction.

CREATURE FEATURE

Imagine you woke up one morning and found that you had switched places with a creature. You may be an insect, a mammal, a reptile, or even a sea creature. Imagine a day in the life of this creature (e.g., what it feels like in the skin of this creature, how your senses have changed, things that are hard to get used to, the best things about being this creature). Write a story about your day as this creature, and include true facts about your chosen creature.

THE LAND OF THE LOST

Imagine that you are a passenger on a bus. It can be any type of bus (e.g., a school bus, a city bus, a Greyhound bus). You are riding along, half asleep, when the bus driver suddenly announces, "Last stop! Everyone off." You're very confused. This is not your stop. You get off the bus, the doors slam closed behind you, and the bus speeds away. You take a look at your surroundings, and you can't believe your eyes. Write a story about where you ended up.

WHO ARE YOU?

For a single day, you are given the opportunity to be someone else. It can be anyone (e.g., a movie star, a comic book hero, a teacher, a character from a novel). This is going to be an exciting day, a day that is out of the ordinary for you, a day that you will be talking about for a long time. Write a journal entry about your day as someone else.

✦ Bonus ✦

Pitch Your Own Project Idea for potential teacher approval.

Tell It Like It Is

Choose one activity to complete.

AN ALIEN ENCOUNTER

Imagine one day, you look out the window and see a spacecraft land right before your eyes. Something out of your control draws you outside and toward the spacecraft. As you stand before the spacecraft, its door opens, and to your great surprise, you find an alien standing there that is nothing like the pictures and drawings of aliens that you have seen in movies and books. You summon all of your courage and walk toward it. Write a newspaper article about your encounter with this alien.

BEHIND CLOSED DOORS

Imagine that a poster hanging on a wall in your classroom falls off, and there behind it, you see a small door. The teacher says it's nothing and quickly covers it back up, but you are extremely curious, and you want answers. During the lunch period, when everyone is in the lunchroom, you sneak back to the classroom. Quickly, before you change your mind, you remove the object covering the door and try the knob. It's not locked, so you quickly open it and go in. Write a tall tale about what you found behind the secret door. You may include visuals to go with your tall tale.

IT'S AN INFERNO

You are sitting at home watching your favorite TV show when the phone rings. You answer the phone and find that it's a reverse 911 call. The operator says, "There is a quickly moving fire in the vicinity. You must evacuate your home immediately. Officers will arrive in 10 minutes to assist you to safety." You look outside, and sure enough, you see a large wall of flames moving in your direction. You alert your family, and you all leap into action. The family will only be able to take what will fit in the car, along with all family members. Explain what you choose to save and why you picked these particular items.

YOU'RE A SUPERHERO!

You were born to an unusual family with unique superpowers. You have never shown others your special powers up until now, when a group of older kids approach you and your friends on the playground and start pushing you around. You can't take it anymore and decide it's time to show your superpowers. Write an account of what happened and the end result. Keep it kid-friendly please.

 **Bonus**

Pitch Your Own Project Idea for potential teacher approval.

SHOW THE WORLD

Choose one activity to complete.

All Wrapped Up
If you were a caterpillar in a cocoon, what would you see, hear, taste, feel, and smell? Write five diary entries sharing your thoughts, feelings, dreams, and so on.

Graph It
Use a variety of graphs (e.g., pie graph, bar graph, picture graph) to tell a story (e.g., your soccer season, the story of your family, injuries you've had).

Pangaea
Pangaea was a continent that many think existed about 250 million years ago. It was at the time when all of the continents were clustered together into one gigantic land mass. What if the continents had not drifted apart? Make a picture book showing the impact this would have on civilization today.

Passport, Please!
Pick an explorer and create a passport for him or her that includes all of the places the person visited. Include a cover, a picture of the explorer, stamp markings, and other items found in an actual passport. View passports to help you with this project.

 Bonus

Pitch Your Own Project Idea for potential teacher approval.

Nursery Rhymes

Get the Baby Out of the Tree

Rock-a-bye baby, on the treetop.
When the wind blows, the cradle will rock.
When the bough breaks, the cradle will fall,
And down will come baby, cradle and all.

Why do we sing this? What is the message? Find out the origin of this lullaby and create a new, more appropriate lullaby to sing to a sleepy baby.

Don't Spill the Water!

Jack and Jill went up the hill
To fetch a pail of water;
Jack fell down and broke his crown,
And Jill came tumbling after.

Then what happened? Write a script and act it out.

Falling Apart

Humpty Dumpty
Sat on a wall;
Humpty Dumpty
Had a great fall;
All the king's horses
And all the king's men
Couldn't put Humpty
Together again.

Why was Humpty on the wall? What made him fall? Who is responsible for this? Write a whodunit mystery about this incident.

Bah, Bah

Mary had a little lamb;
Its fleece was white as snow;
And everywhere that Mary went,
The lamb was sure to go.

It followed her to school one day,
Which was against the rule.
It made the children laugh and shout
To see a lamb at school.

Rewrite "Mary Had a Little Lamb" so that Mary has a new animal that she takes somewhere other than to school.

Bonus

Pitch Your Own Project Idea for potential teacher approval.

Choose one activity to complete.

SO MANY QUESTIONS

THE BERMUDA TRIANGLE

What is the Bermuda Triangle? Gather facts about the Bermuda Triangle, and write a ship captain's log with facts, findings, curiosities, and a final SOS.

HELEN KELLER

Who was Helen Keller? Write a diary as if Helen Keller had written it herself. Include major events in her life along with a visual timeline.

THE MAYFLOWER

The *Mayflower* set sail from England in 1620. Research the *Mayflower*'s journey and create journal entries from a pilgrim telling about the journey and the pilgrim's hopes, fears, and dreams. Include a map of the route of the *Mayflower*'s journey.

THE UNDERGROUND RAILROAD

Was the Underground Railroad a real railroad? Make a map of its route and write a letter from the point of view of a runaway slave. Include his or her hopes, fears, and dreams.

CHOOSE ONE ACTIVITY TO COMPLETE.

 **Bonus**

Pitch Your Own Project Idea for potential teacher approval.

How It Came to Be

CHOOSE ONE ACTIVITY TO COMPLETE.

SHOW ME THOSE DIMPLES

Why are there dimples on a golf ball? First come up with a fable explaining how the golf ball got its dimples. Then look up the real answer. Make sure to include both the moral of your story and the real answer to the question. You should include other media (e.g., visuals, music, displays, computer graphics).

SHINE ON

Why does the moon shine? First come up with a fable explaining why the moon shines. Then look up the real answer. Make sure to include both the moral of your story and the real answer to the question. You should include other media (e.g., visuals, music, displays, computer graphics).

IT'S NOT JUST A CANDY BAR

Why is our galaxy called The Milky Way? First come up with a fable explaining how our galaxy got its name. Then look up the real answer. Make sure to include both the moral of your story and the real answer to the question. You should include other media (e.g., visuals, music, displays, computer graphics).

CRACKING UP

Why is the Liberty Bell cracked? First come up with a fable explaining how the Liberty Bell got cracked. Then look up the real answer. Make sure to include both the moral of your story and the real answer to the question. You should include other media (e.g., visuals, music, displays, computer graphics).

✦ Bonus ✦

Pitch Your Own Project Idea for potential teacher approval.

Persuasive Communications

DOI: 10.4324/9781003529316-10

It's All About School

Choose one activity to complete.

THE CHOICE IS YOURS

Your school principal is going to grant your whole grade one privilege. It is a privilege that the other grades in your school will not have. It must be a real possibility, something doable. Think of one privilege that you would like to have and why your class alone should be granted this privilege. Draft a petition designed to convince the principal to grant this privilege. Think about some arguments in favor of this privilege.

WE'VE GOT CLASS

It is the first day of the school year. When you arrive at school, you find that there is a new class being offered. It's a class that's never been offered before at your school, or at any other school that you know of. Think of a class that you don't have in your school—a class that would be out of the ordinary at most schools, but a class that has value and that you feel is important for students to experience. Write a letter to convince your school and community that this class is necessary to a student's education. Support your ideas with examples and details.

✦ Bonus ✦
Pitch Your Own Project
Idea for potential
teacher approval.

IT'S ALL FUN AND GAMES

Your principal has just made an announcement. There has been a very large donation given to the school to go toward updating the school playground. The students have been asked to design an awesome playground that has something for everyone. Anything goes, but the playground should be able to fit on the school grounds. Write an essay describing your playground and swaying others to select your playground rather than the others submitted. Supply blueprints of your playground design.

FOOD FOR THOUGHT

The principal has decided that the school lunchroom is in desperate need of a makeover. He or she feels there's nobody better qualified to design the lunchroom than the students themselves. You have been asked to design an awesome lunchroom from top to bottom, and anything goes. Think about color, furniture, food, and additions to the current lunchroom. Make a model of the new lunchroom and write a letter to your principal trying to convince him or her to make the changes. Support your ideas with examples and details.

GOOD NEWS!

Choose one activity to complete.

News Flash

Your local news station is holding auditions. It is looking to hire a student reporter to present a special feature that others your age would like to see as part of the news program. You get to come up with this special feature, and it can have any focus (e.g., zoo animals, young heroes, special events). Any idea is acceptable, as long as it is informative and would be enjoyed by others your age. You will have a lot of competition for this job, so your idea should be as unique as possible. Create a resume and write an essay to convince your local TV station to hire you as its student reporter.

A Redesign

You've been asking forever, and finally you are getting permission to make changes to your bedroom. Think about what you would do (e.g., add color, change furnishings, make additions). Draw a diagram of your new bedroom design. Then, write a letter to your parents trying to convince them to make the changes. Support your ideas with examples and details both visual and written.

No Place Like Home

Your family feels it is time for a change. They want to move, and they have given you two choices: either move to the city, or move to the country. Think about where you would like to be and what place would be best for your family. Create a real estate listing about the place that you feel the family should settle. Give at least three reasons to support your choice.

Thriller

Think of an activity that may be a bit dangerous, but that is something you would really like to do (e.g., rock climbing, sky diving, bungee jumping). Now, write an essay pleading your case. Include facts and statistics about your chosen activity.

 **Bonus** Pitch Your Own Project Idea for potential teacher approval.

FAIRY TALE TROUBLES

Choose one activity to complete.

Get Out of Our House!

Read the story *Goldilocks and the Three Bears*. Do you believe that Goldilocks did anything wrong? Could Goldilocks have committed a crime? Think about the facts in the story and write a persuasive essay for or against Goldilocks.

A Nasty Boy!

Read the story *Jack and the Beanstalk*. Look at the criminal behavior Jack could be charged with (e.g., possible robbery, possible murder) and make a formal speech convincing others of Jack's guilt.

Don't Be Jealous

Read the story *Snow White and the Seven Dwarfs*. Write a letter from Snow White's stepmother to the "Dear Abby" advice column asking for advice about what to do about her jealous rage against Snow White. Then write a response from Abby pleading with the queen to let those feeling go. Include suggestions on what the queen can do when these jealous rages arise.

Pork Chops for Dinner!

Read the story *The Three Little Pigs*. Design a homemade security system that will make the pigs safer. Describe the system and write an advertisement persuading the pigs to buy your product.

✦ Bonus ✦

Pitch Your Own Project Idea for potential teacher approval.

A Fairy Tale Fix

Choose one activity to complete.

Order in the Court

Read the story *Little Red Riding Hood*. The wolf committed quite a few crimes, and you have been selected to try him in court for his crimes. Think about the facts in the story and write your closing statement, telling the jury what the wolf is being accused of and pleading your case against him.

Please Don't Eat!

Read the story *The Gingerbread Boy*. Set up a demonstration (with signs and slogans) designed to convince others not to eat the Gingerbread Boy. Make your signs and slogans clever and on point (like Chick-fil-A "Eat More Chicken" campaign). Gather some classmates to help you stage your demonstration.

And Away They Go!

Read the story *The Pied Piper of Hamelin*. Not only did the Pied Piper of Hamelin get rid of the rats, but when he wasn't paid for his services, he also got rid of the children. Write an essay persuading the townspeople that the mayor was wrong in not paying the Pied Piper. Then create a "Lost" flier for the missing children.

Beauty Is Only Skin Deep

Read the story *The Ugly Duckling*. Write a rap about the prejudice against the duckling and the meaning of the word beauty.

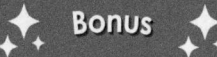

Bonus

Pitch Your Own Project Idea for potential teacher approval.

What Do You Think?

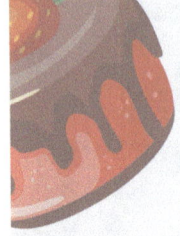

A New Holiday

December 21 is National Flashlight Day. What new national holiday would you start? Write a persuasive argument in favor of this new national holiday and design a petition to see if other students would like to celebrate your new holiday.

School Event

Many schools have special events like book fairs, ice cream socials, and talent shows. What new event would you like to bring to your school? Anything goes so be creative. Write and deliver a persuasive speech describing your new event.

Man Overboard

In a disaster like the sinking of the Titanic, who should be saved first? Research what the crew and passengers did on the Titanic when it was sinking, and then write a persuasive essay on what policy you think all large ships should implement. Include a pamphlet that shows procedural steps for evacuation.

You Rule!

If you could make one rule that everyone in your school had to follow, what rule would you make? Why? Write a letter to the principal stating your rule and why it should be implemented at your school. Create a poster to advertise your new rule.

✦ **Bonus** ✦

Pitch Your Own Project Idea for potential teacher approval.

Choose one activity to complete.

TOPICS TO DEBATE

Choose an activity to complete.

BANNED BOOKS

Charlotte's Web was banned in some school districts because the story portrayed talking animals that can communicate and act just like humans. Do you agree or disagree with the actions of banning books in school libraries? Design a presentation to get your point across.

DON'T SHOOT

Parents are looking for advice on whether or not they should purchase toy guns for their children. Do some research on this topic, and then write an advice column on whether parents should or should not purchase toy guns for children.

 Bonus

Pitch Your Own Project Idea for potential teacher approval.

TEACHER VS. STUDENT

Would you rather be the teacher or the student? Start by making a pros and cons list for each. Then design an award and prepare a speech dedicated to your choice.

LOOK ALIKE

Are you for or against school uniforms? Write a persuasive rap that is either pro-uniforms or anti-uniforms.

Expository Communications

DOI: 10.4324/9781003529316-11

It's Up To You

Into the Future

Citizens of your city are putting together a time capsule for future generations, and they want to include important items that represent the culture of your time period (e.g., music, technology, the arts, sciences). Each citizen can submit one item to possibly be included in the time capsule. You have a lot of competition, so make sure you pick something that is unique and that you feel future generations should know about. Convince the committee sponsoring the time capsule to include your item, explaining thoroughly the item's use and significance.

ROCKET MAN

You are an astronaut on a peaceful exploratory mission to a newly discovered planet. As a representative from Earth, you are to present two gifts from our planet. You are to select gifts that represent our planet, are meaningful to those on our planet, and are valuable to those on the newly discovered planet. Make a greeting card explaining the two gifts you are giving and their significance to those on Earth.

Choose an activity to complete.

Earth Day

Does your school celebrate Earth day? Come up with an activity (make bird feeders, pick up trash, make art with recycled materials, etc.) and write a letter to your teacher or principal explaining how this activity will inspire students and make a difference.

UNPLUGGED

Imagine that you have no TV, cell phone, computer, tablet, video games or other technology for one week! Think about how this would affect your daily life. Now think of some activities that you can do, instead, to keep you busy and out of trouble. They can be activities that you've never tried or wish you could do more often. Anything goes, as long as you stay away from the electronics. Write an essay to explain what you can do to keep occupied in a week of no technology. Support your ideas with examples and details.

Bonus
Pitch Your Own Project Idea for potential teacher approval.

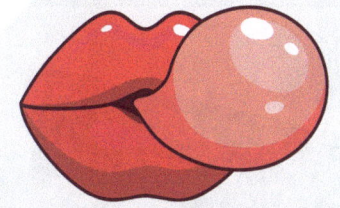

Present It Out Loud

FREAKY FRIDAY

Imagine that today you can change places with anyone you would like. This person can be real or imaginary, from the past or from the present. Write and perform a speech explaining why you wanted to change places with that person and what events take place during the switched-identity day.

CHA-CHING!

Congratulations! You have just won a million dollars in the lottery. Once you calm down, you realize that you have some serious thinking to do. A million dollars is a lot of money, and it's your responsibility to figure out just what to do with all of that money. It can change your life for the better, or it can make your life worse. Present a monologue showing your reaction upon hearing that you won a million dollars and your thoughts on what you will do with the money that you have just won. Perform your monologue for the class.

 Bonus

Pitch Your Own Project Idea for potential teacher approval.

LIFE IS A HIGHWAY

You are in desperate need of a getaway. You want to go to your absolute favorite place. It can be a place where you've actually been, or a place that you know a lot about and have always wanted to visit. The problem is, you need to convince your parents to take you there or let you go there. Create a video or online slideshow presentation to convince your parents to make your dream a reality.

PET PROJECT

You've been asking forever, and finally your parents are going to let you get a pet. Not just an ordinary pet, but something unusual (e.g., a reptile from the rainforest, a marsupial from down under, an aquatic animal from the Great Barrier Reef). Think about how life will change with this new pet and what you will need to do to your environment to help this pet thrive. Write a convincing argument stating why this pet will be perfect for you and your family. Support your ideas with examples and details.

Choose an activity to complete.

SHOW YOUR STUFF

CHOOSE ONE ACTIVITY TO COMPLETE.

Stamp of Approval

The U.S. Postal Service has honored many individuals by placing their portraits on postage stamps. There have been presidents, singers, Olympic athletes, astronauts, and even cartoon characters featured on stamps. Think about whom you would nominate with a postage stamp and the reasons why this person should have his or her own stamp. Create this new postage stamp and write an essay telling why you honored this individual with a stamp.

The Perfect Sibling

Imagine that you could "invent" the perfect sibling: the brother or sister you have always wished for. Think about whether this person would be a boy or a girl, older or younger. Think about the qualities that would make him or her the perfect sibling. Write a description of this perfect sibling in the form of a poem or a memoir.

You Plan-It!

Off in the distance, there is a planet. You are the very first visitor to step foot on this planet. There are three important things that you will notice on this new planet: you will notice the climate on the planet, you will notice the planet's landscape, and finally, you will discover what lives on this planet. Create a piece of news footage of you on this planet telling what it's like there.

Throw It Away

The landfills are overloaded, and the government is putting out a plea to the people. They need your ideas. What would you do with all of the world's garbage? Create a digital message (e.g., blog, Instagram post, text messages) stating the problem and presenting your solution.

✦ **Bonus** ✦

Pitch Your Own Project Idea for potential teacher approval.

Our World

Be Prepared

What items would you put in an emergency bag to keep in your car during the summer months? What about a bag during the winter months? Make a display or give a demonstration showing items needed in the summer and winter emergency bags and write an essay convincing others of the importance of keeping similar bags in their cars.

Send It to Space

What if all of our garbage was launched into space? What would be both the positive and negative effects? Write an essay stating both the pros and the cons and lead a classroom debate on this topic.

A Grave Situation

What would happen if we had 10% less gravity on Earth? Think about transportation, sports, nature, and other issues. Write an essay describing what effects a decrease in gravity would have on our life and include illustrations showing these effects.

Weather or Not

What if the weather never changed and instead always stayed the same (e.g., cold/hot, wet/dry, windy/calm)? It would be always the same, day in and day out. Write an essay on the effect of weather that never changes on humans and nature and deliver a weather report for the evening news.

Bonus

Pitch Your Own Project Idea for potential teacher approval.

Choose one activity to complete.

Explain, Please

Choose one activity to complete.

DESIGN A STATUE

The Statue of Liberty was a gift that now resides in the New York Harbor. Look up its history and meaning. Design a statue for your town and explain its meaning. Include a model of your statue.

WHO SHALL PAY?

If a child commits a crime, should the parents do the time? Start a blog, podcast, or debate on this topic, asking for not only a yes or no answer, but for the respondents' reasoning. Graph the results of this conversation or debate.

THE OLYMPIC RINGS

What do the five Olympic rings mean? Explain their meaning, and create an additional Olympic ring, the meaning of which you should explain. Include an illustration showing how the additional ring will fit in with the existing five rings.

FLY AWAY

Write and present a monologue about what it would be like if you woke up one morning with wings.

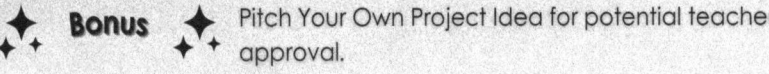

✦ **Bonus** ✦ Pitch Your Own Project Idea for potential teacher approval.

Find Out

Old Glory

What do the colors red, white, and blue symbolize in the American flag? Explain the colors' origins, and then share what three colors you feel symbolize you. Write a song or a poem to showcase your thoughts.

Seven Wonders of the World

What are the seven wonders of the world? Create a short-form video, or online slideshow that includes the seven wonders, along with an explanation of what you feel should be the eighth wonder of the world.

Drowning in Quicksand

Why does quicksand make you sink? Explain how quicksand works and tell about at least 10 other unusual phenomena found in our world. Present the information in whatever way you like (e.g., speech, slideshow, visual display).

The Highest in the World

What is the highest waterfall in the world? Create an exhibit that includes facts on this waterfall, along with facts on 10 other "highests" in the world—buildings, mountains, statues, and so on.

Choose one activity to complete.

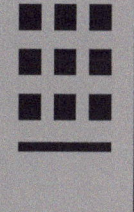

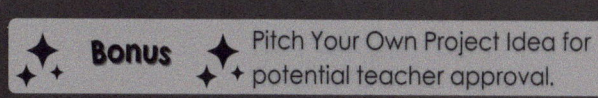

Bonus Pitch Your Own Project Idea for potential teacher approval.

References

Career and Technical Education (CTE). (2024). *21st century skills.*

Colorado Department of Education. (2020). Colorado academic standards. Denver, CO: Author.

International Reading Association, & National Council of Teachers of English. (Reaffirmed 2012). *Standards for the English language arts.* Retrieved from http://www.ncte.org/library/NCTEFiles/Resources/Books/Sample/StandardsDoc.pdf

Tomlinson, C. A. (1999). *The differentiated classroom: Responding to the needs of all learners.* Alexandria, VA: Association for Supervision and Curriculum Development.

Common Core State Standards

Preparing America's Students for College and Career (NGA Center and CCSSO 2009)

Comprehension and Collaboration:

CCSS.ELA-Literacy.CCRA.SL.1
Prepare for and participate effectively in a range of conversations and collaborations with diverse partners, building on others' ideas and expressing their own clearly and persuasively.
CCSS.ELA-Literacy.CCRA.SL.2
Integrate and evaluate information presented in diverse media and formats, including visually, quantitatively, and orally.

CCSS.ELA-Literacy.CCRA.SL.3

Evaluate a speaker's point of view, reasoning, and use of evidence and rhetoric.

Presentation of Knowledge and Ideas:

CCSS.ELA-Literacy.CCRA.SL.4

Present information, findings, and supporting evidence such that listeners can follow the line of reasoning and the organization, development, and style are appropriate to task, purpose, and audience.

CCSS.ELA-Literacy.CCRA.SL.5

Make strategic use of digital media and visual displays of data to express information and enhance understanding of presentations.

CCSS.ELA-Literacy.CCRA.SL.6

Adapt speech to a variety of contexts and communicative tasks, demonstrating command of formal English when indicated or appropriate.

Integration of Knowledge and Ideas:

CCSS.ELA-Literacy.CCRA.R.7

Integrate and evaluate content presented in diverse media and formats, including visually and quantitatively, as well as in words.

CCSS.ELA-Literacy.CCRA.R.8

Delineate and evaluate the argument and specific claims in a text, including the validity of the reasoning as well as the relevance and sufficiency of the evidence.

CCSS.ELA-Literacy.CCRA.R.9

Analyze how two or more texts address similar themes or topics in order to build knowledge or to compare the approaches the authors take.

Text Types and Purposes:

CCSS.ELA-Literacy.CCRA.W.1

Write arguments to support claims in an analysis of substantive topics or texts using valid reasoning and relevant and sufficient evidence.

CCSS.ELA-Literacy.CCRA.W.2

Write informative/explanatory texts to examine and convey complex ideas and information clearly and accurately through the effective selection, organization, and analysis of content.

CCSS.ELA-Literacy.CCRA.W.3

Write narratives to develop real or imagined experiences or events using effective technique, well-chosen details and well-structured event sequences.

Production and Distribution of Writing:

CCSS.ELA-Literacy.CCRA.W.4

Produce clear and coherent writing in which the development, organization, and style are appropriate to task, purpose, and audience.

CCSS.ELA-Literacy.CCRA.W.5

Develop and strengthen writing as needed by planning, revising, editing, rewriting, or trying a new approach.

CCSS.ELA-Literacy.CCRA.W.6

Use technology, including the Internet, to produce and publish writing and to interact and collaborate with others.

Research to Build and Present Knowledge:

CCSS.ELA-Literacy.CCRA.W.7

Conduct short as well as more sustained research projects based on focused questions, demonstrating understanding of the subject under investigation.

CCSS.ELA-Literacy.CCRA.W.8

Gather relevant information from multiple print and digital sources, assess the credibility and accuracy of each source, and integrate the information while avoiding plagiarism.

CCSS.ELA-Literacy.CCRA.W.9

Draw evidence from literary or informational texts to support analysis, reflection, and research.

Conventions of Standard English:

CCSS.ELA-Literacy.CCRA.L.1

Demonstrate command of the conventions of standard English grammar and usage when writing or speaking.

CCSS.ELA-Literacy.CCRA.L.2

Demonstrate command of the conventions of standard English capitalization, punctuation, and spelling when writing.

Knowledge of Language:

CCSS.ELA-Literacy.CCRA.L.3

Apply knowledge of language to understand how language functions in different contexts, to make effective choices for meaning or style, and to comprehend more fully when reading or listening.